Judy Lee
A gift for

Thanks for the
wonderful Tea for Tasha!
From Pat

Published by the J. Countryman division of the
Thomas Nelson Book Group, Nashville, Tennessee 37214.

Project editor—Terri Gibbs

Designed by LeftCoast Design, Portland, Oregon.

ISBN: 1-4041-0028-8

www.thomasnelson.com • www.jcountryman.com

Printed and bound in China

Thank you to Marjorie for her homespun help!

Dedicated to Joyce,
the Queen of Comfort,
who sews a smile,
quilts a laugh,
then hems with love
to make it last.

A heart-felt thanks to Reba Starling,
owner of The Shoppe at Shady
Gables® in Versailles, Missouri, for
her many teatime inspirations
and for the quiet afternoons
spent taking tea in her
lovely tea room.

the shoppe at
SHADY GABLES

TEA

Above all things put on love.

Colossians 3:14

Introduction

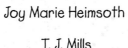

Tea and friendship are two of the nicest words, and when you bring them together in the nourishment of heart and soul, . . . well, that's exactly why tea parties got started! Even as little girls, we instinctively knew that if we gathered together all the "friends" we could find from our toy box and propped them up for tea and cookies and a giggle or two, a good time was sure to be had by all.

Chatting together over a cup of tea is such a friendly thing to do. Who can say which brings the most comfort—the warm tea or the warm heart of a friend? When we share our heart with another, we discover the good becomes better and the bad becomes manageable.

Life is sprinkled with golden opportunities to bless others with the friendly gesture of tea. Why not have a Mother's Day Tea, a Christmas Tea, or a simple country style Friendship Tea? We hope this collection of warm-hearted inspirations, comforting prayers, party ideas, and taste-tempting recipes will inspire you to create your own TEATIME TREASURES!

Joy Marie Heimsoth

T. J. Mills

The warmth I feel
from a party with tea
comes not from the drink,
but the friends I see.

Close to my heart you'll always be; friends forever you and me.

 Friendship is where we go to sing of happiness or cry over sorrow, to share laughter and tears. And then there's tea! How many faithful friendships can be blamed on tea?

There's no need to wait for a date on the calendar. Gather your friends together for tea … and do it as often as you like! Eat, drink, and discuss trivial things that are valuable only because they're so silly! Tell old stories about each other and laugh till your sides hurt. Share together, pray together, and bless each other.

Friendship feeds the spirit and lifts the heart. So take time to enjoy good tea with good friends. It will bring balance and blessings to your heart. Indulge! Grab life by the teacup and don't let go until the last scone is gone, and you have sweetened your tea with the comfort of kindness.

 Nonsense among friends makes perfect sense!

A Garden Tea Party

The golden warmth of a summer day is a great setting for a garden tea party. The suggested tea would be flavored ice tea. Brew a large amount of iced tea ahead of time and serve it in carafes at the table.

Using a stockpot, bring two gallons of cold water to a boil and add eight tablespoons of loose tea (regular black or flavored if you prefer). Remove from heat and stir until all tea leaves are moist. Place lid back on the stockpot and allow it to steep for eight minutes. Stir the leaves once more before straining the tea into pitchers. (Do not pour the hot tea directly into a glass pitcher as it might break.) Allow plenty of time for tea to chill before serving. Season with mint leaves, orange or lemon peel shavings, or a bit of your favorite berry juice.

Serve dainty sandwiches made from your favorite fillings and don't forget to pass plates of delicious desserts. To protect the luscious plates of sandwiches and goodies from outdoor pests, cover them with tulle in a beautiful variety of colors.

Everything grows better with love.

A Friendship Prayer

Bless my friends
For they are gold;
The riches of my heart and soul.
May I be worthy of such
A treasure
And ever thankful
For this pleasure.

Amen

Bread Basket

This edible masterpiece is a woven delight that is almost too pretty to eat!

2 loaves frozen bread dough, thawed
1 beaten egg

Preheat oven to 350-degrees. Invert two 2-qt. oven-proof bowls on a large cookie sheet. Cover with aluminum foil, molding to sides. Roll each loaf of dough into a 10" x 13" rectangle and cut in 1" strips. Braid 3 strips for the handle and place over one of the foil covered bowls. With the remaining strips, wrap the dough around the other foil-covered bowl. Bake 20 minutes. Remove from oven and brush with beaten egg. Return to oven and bake an additional 8 minutes, or until a deep golden brown. Cool completely. Remove bowl and carefully remove the foil. Attach the handle to sides of the bowl with tooth-picks. Add decorative ribbon to handle and line the basket with fabric. Fill with muffins.

A friend loves at all times.
Proverbs 17:17

Poppy Seed Muffins

These glazed little glories are perfect with a warm cup of tea

3 cups flour
1 1/2 tsp. baking powder
2 cups sugar
1 1/2 tsp. poppy seeds
1 1/2 tsp. almond flavoring
1 1/2 tsp. butter flavoring

1 tsp. salt
3 eggs
1 1/2 cups milk
1 1/8 cup oil
1 1/2 tsp. vanilla flavoring

Mix ingredients together and fill paper-lined muffin tins 2/3 full. Bake 325-degrees for 15 minutes. Makes 30 muffins.

Glaze:
1 cup powdered sugar
1/2 tsp. butter flavoring
1/2 tsp. vanilla flavoring

1/4 cup orange juice
1/2 tsp. almond flavoring

Mix together and spoon over hot muffins.

Friendship is God's special way of loving us through someone else.
–Anonymous

Recipe for Friendship

Quiet time together
Frequent shopping trips
Tea for two
Three phone calls a week

Stir ingredients with a gentle touch.
Sprinkle with understanding,
a dash of encouragement, and
a pinch of laughter.
Bake slowly in the warmth
of memories.
Enjoy for a lifetime.

Margi

Aunt Marie's Brownies

These moist, fluffy cake-like brownies are the perfect chocolate treat. Great with a fruit flavored tea.

2 cups sugar
2 cups flour
1/2 tsp. salt
1 tsp. baking soda

1 stick butter
1 cup water
1/4 cup cocoa
1/2 cup vegetable oil

1/2 cup buttermilk
2 eggs
1/4 tsp. burnt sugar flavoring
1 tsp. vanilla

Sift dry ingredients together and set aside in large bowl. In medium sauce pan, cook butter, water, cocoa, and oil just to a boil. Stir this mixture into the dry ingredients. Add buttermilk, eggs, and flavorings and stir until well blended. Pour into greased 11x17 pan. Bake in a 350-degree oven for 25 minutes. Cool completely before frosting.

Frosting:
1/4 cup butter, melted
1/4 cup buttermilk

2 Tbsp. cocoa
1/2 tsp. vanilla

2 cups powdered sugar

Sift cocoa and powdered sugar together in small mixing bowl. Add butter, buttermilk, and vanilla and stir until well blended. Frost brownies and let set before cutting.

—Margi

 Friends and chocolate go hand in hand so why not
have a tea party with a chocolate theme? It's nurturing you can taste!

Chocolate Dream

You'll think you're dreaming when you bite into one of these delicacies, but they're all real and completely delicious!

Mini crust:
- 1 chocolate cake mix
- 1 egg
- 1 stick butter, melted

Combine ingredients together for crust. Roll into 1" balls and press into a mini muffin tin. Bake 9 minutes in a 325-degree oven. Cool completely.

Filling:

- 1 1/4 cup sugar
- 3/4 cup butter
- 4 ounces unsweetened chocolate, melted and cooled
- 1 tsp. vanilla
- 3 eggs
- 1 container whipped topping (8 oz.)

Beat sugar and butter with an electric mixer until fluffy. Stir in chocolate and vanilla. Add eggs, one at a time, beating on high after each addition. Fold in whipped topping and spoon filling into prepared crusts. Chill until ready to serve.

A friend who cares, will always be there, ready and waiting with chocolate to share.

Chocolate Chip Tea Biscuits

4 cups bread flour
2 Tbsp. baking powder
1 cup mini chocolate chips
1 cup evaporated milk

¹/₄ cup sugar
¹/₂ tsp. salt
4 eggs, (save 1 for glaze)
1 ¹/₂ tsp. vanilla

¹/₄ cup brown sugar
¹/₂ cup cold butter

Combine dry ingredients in large bowl. With pastry blender, cut in butter until mixture resembles coarse crumbs. Stir in morsels. In a separate dish beat 3 eggs, milk, and vanilla. Add to flour mixture. Stir until soft dough forms. Pat dough to three-quarter inch thickness on flour-covered wax paper. Cut with one-and-a-half-inch biscuit cutter. Place on lightly greased baking sheet. Beat 1 egg and brush over biscuits. Bake in 325-degree oven for 12 minutes or until golden brown. Remove to wire racks and serve warm.

Chocolate contains phenyl ethylamine (PEA) a natural substance that stimulates the same reaction in the body as falling in love! So sharing chocolate is kind of like sharing love.

Teatime Tidbits

Anna, the seventh Duchess of Bedford, first practiced the fine tradition of "afternoon tea," in an effort to satisfy her afternoon hunger. In those times, dinner was served rather late in the day and she was in need of something to hold her over. She then turned it into a social occasion by inviting her friends over to share this afternoon treat and needless to say, it caught on!

Victorian women were known to be so serious about taking their afternoon tea that when invited out for tea, they would bring their own cup and saucer wrapped carefully in a special box!

There are three kinds of tea: black, green, and oolong. The difference is in how the tea leaves are processed. Black tea leaves are fermented fully, green tea leaves are not fermented at all, and oolong tea leaves are partially fermented.

The table's all set
With lots of pretty things.
The kettle's on the stove
And soon will sing.
We're all gathered 'round
For a warm friendly tea
And to enjoy one another
So delightfully.

A Mother's Day
Tea

It's all about Love.

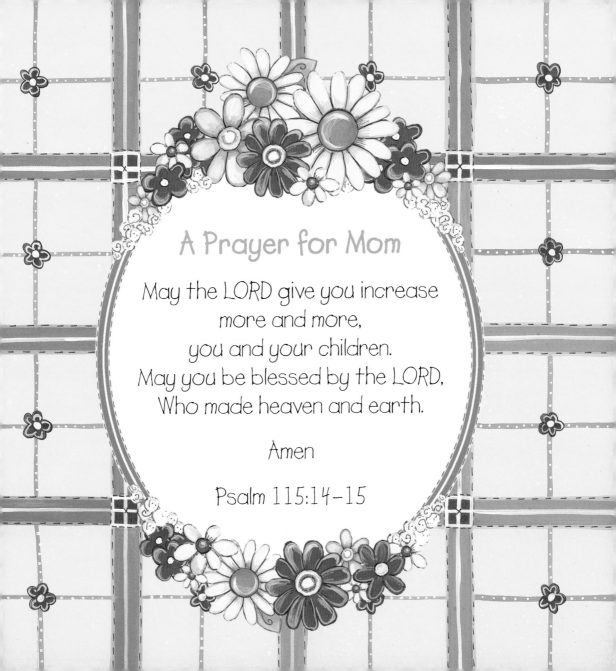

A Prayer for Mom

May the LORD give you increase
more and more,
you and your children.
May you be blessed by the LORD,
Who made heaven and earth.

Amen

Psalm 115:14–15

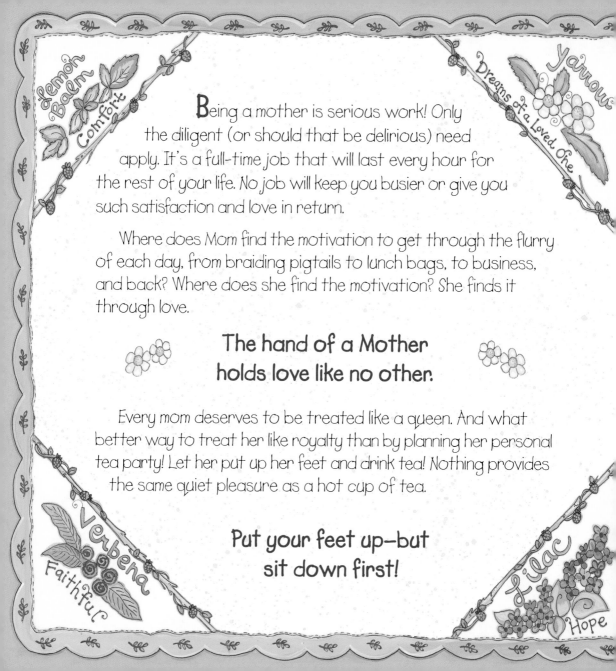

Lemon Balm — Comfort

Yarrow

Dreams of a Loved One

Being a mother is serious work! Only the diligent (or should that be delirious) need apply. It's a full-time job that will last every hour for the rest of your life. No job will keep you busier or give you such satisfaction and love in return.

Where does Mom find the motivation to get through the flurry of each day, from braiding pigtails to lunch bags, to business, and back? Where does she find the motivation? She finds it through love.

The hand of a Mother holds love like no other.

Every mom deserves to be treated like a queen. And what better way to treat her like royalty than by planning her personal tea party! Let her put up her feet and drink tea! Nothing provides the same quiet pleasure as a hot cup of tea.

Put your feet up—but sit down first!

Verbena — Faithful

Lilac — Hope

Nourish the soul
with goodness
and light,
reflect in the joy
of teatime delights.

Chamomile

Patience

A cup of tea
to chase the gloom
'till flowers on
the prairie bloom.

Thyme

Courage

A spot of
gentle comfort
Is waiting just for me,
In my chair beside
the window
With a book and
cup of tea.

Pansies

Happiness

A cup of tea
in time
leaves worry
and care behind.
—Dulcy

Violet

Joy

While all around
the world spins
I'll sip my tea
'till it stops again.

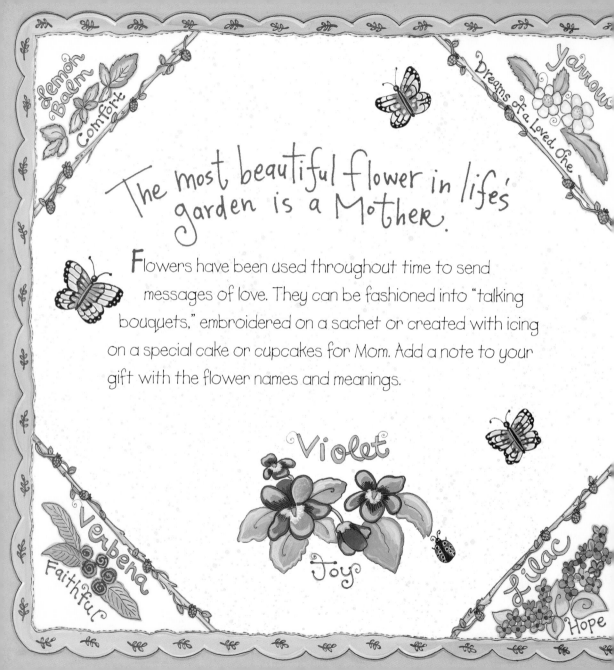

The most beautiful flower in life's garden is a Mother.

Flowers have been used throughout time to send messages of love. They can be fashioned into "talking bouquets," embroidered on a sachet or created with icing on a special cake or cupcakes for Mom. Add a note to your gift with the flower names and meanings.

Lemon Balm — Comfort

Yarrow — Dreams of a Loved One

Violet — Joy

Verbena — Faithful

Lilac — Hope

Flowers for Mother's Day

Lemon Mint–Joyful
Purple Coneflower–Skill
Geranium Leaf–Comfort
Bee Balm–Consideration
Baby's Breath–Pure Heart
Lemon Balm–Playfulness
Rosemary–Devotion
Sunflower–Adoration
Sage–Appreciation
Forget-Me-Not–Hope
Rosebud–Tenderness
Lily–Beauty

Lemon Balm Comfort

Yarrow
Dreams of a Loved One

Thyme
Courage

Chamomile
Patience

Verbena
Faithful

Pansies
Happiness

Lilac
Hope

Mother's Day Tea Menu

Egg Salad Tea Sandwiches

Pecan Cream Cheese Tea Sandwiches

Fresh Strawberries

Sliced Kiwi

Front Porch Scones

Farmhouse Strawberry Jam

Fresh Cream

Lemon Tea Cakes

Blueberry Tea

Apricot-Peach Tea

A visit with Mom
is not complete
'till the teapot
whistles its tune
so sweet!

Here are several quick and easy ways to make the perfect finger sandwiches for a light afternoon tea treat. Make them even more special by cutting out the bread with cookie cutters. Fun and tasty!

Egg Salad
A light and pretty treat!

Chop 8 hard-boiled eggs and add 2/3 cup mayonnaise. Salt and pepper to taste. Mix well and spread on bread that has been lightly toasted. Top with sliced almonds and parsley.

Pecan Cream Cheese Tea Sandwiches

1 package cream cheese, softened (8 oz.)
1 Tbsp. honey
1 cup chopped pecans

Combine all ingredients until well blended. Spread on lightly toasted bread.

Delicate Olive Cream Cheese Spread

1 package cream cheese, softened (8 oz)
$1/2$ cup mayonnaise
$1/2$ cup chopped black olives
2 Tbsp. olive juice
$1/2$ cup finely chopped pecans
dash of pepper

Mix all ingredients well. Refrigerate 4 hours before using. Do not freeze. Keeps well in refrigerator. Good on pumpernickel, rye or whole wheat bread.

Lemon Tea Cakes

Ingredients
1½ cups butter, softened
1 (8 oz.) pkg. cream cheese, softened
2¼ cups sugar
6 eggs
3 Tbsp. lemon juice
1 tsp. vanilla flavoring
1½ tsp. grated lemon peel
3 cups all-purpose flour

Glaze

4½ cups powdered sugar
½ cup half-n-half
3½ tsp. lemon flavoring

In a mixing bowl cream butter, cream cheese and sugar. Add eggs, one at a time, and beat well. Add flavoring and lemon peel. Gradually mix in the flour. Fill paper lined miniature muffin cups 2/3 full. Bake at 325 degrees for 10-15 minutes. While tea cakes are baking, mix the glaze ingredients together in a small bowl. Cool tea cakes 5 minutes, then remove paper cups and dip the tops of the warm tea cakes in glaze. Place on wire rack to cool completely and the glaze dry.

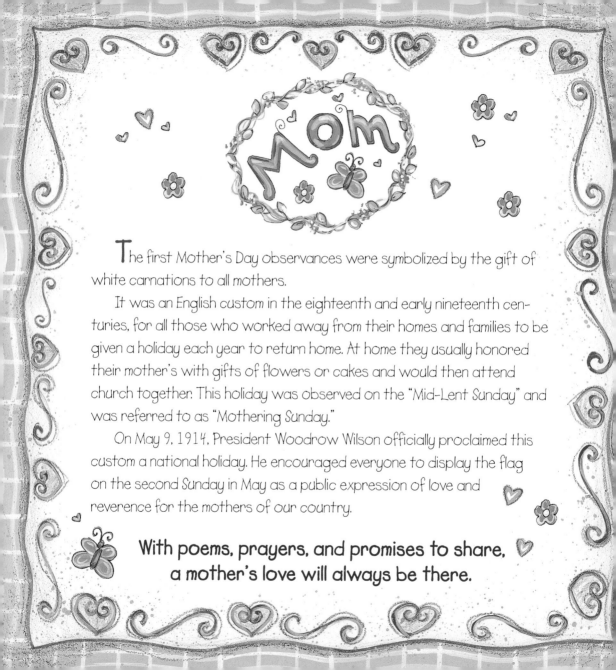

Mom

The first Mother's Day observances were symbolized by the gift of white carnations to all mothers.

It was an English custom in the eighteenth and early nineteenth centuries, for all those who worked away from their homes and families to be given a holiday each year to return home. At home they usually honored their mother's with gifts of flowers or cakes and would then attend church together. This holiday was observed on the "Mid-Lent Sunday" and was referred to as "Mothering Sunday."

On May 9, 1914, President Woodrow Wilson officially proclaimed this custom a national holiday. He encouraged everyone to display the flag on the second Sunday in May as a public expression of love and reverence for the mothers of our country.

**With poems, prayers, and promises to share,
a mother's love will always be there.**

Of all earthly things
God gives,
There is one above
all others;
It is the precious,
priceless gift
of faithful
Christian mothers.

-Anonymous

Mothers & Daughters

Heartstrings tied
with loving care -
A sacred bond
beyond compare.

Let's have a tea
For you and for me.
I'll fetch cup and saucer
While you heat the water.
We'll sit down together
And talk about weather,
Yet not for the talk
Of cool days or hot
but just for the fun.
And when we are done
We'll wash out our cups
And hang them right up
For the next lovely day
When one of us will say
Let's have a tea
for you and for me!

Brewing Tea ... Properly!

It's so easy to dunk a tea bag in a mug of boiling water. But if you want to enjoy the best possible tea, try brewing it the proper, old-fashioned way.

Start by filling the kettle with fresh, cold water. While waiting for the kettle to whistle, fill the teapot (ceramic teapots are best for holding heat) with hot water to warm it. Before the kettle boils, empty the teapot of its "warming water" and add the tea leaves either into a tea sock, infusion basket, or directly into the teapot. Use one teaspoon of loose tea for each cup and as the saying goes, "one more for the pot." (If you are using teabags you should use one teabag less than the number of cups.)

As soon as the kettle whistles, pour the boiling water into the teapot. (Take care not to boil the water too long as this depletes the oxygen in the water and can result in a flat tasting brew.) Place the lid on the teapot and allow it to steep for three to five minutes. Before pouring, gently stir or swirl the tea leaves around inside the teapot. Pour through a strainer into the cup. Remove the tea leaves or teabags to prevent further steeping.

Top off the teapot with a tea cozy to keep the pot warm for the next cup of tea. Enjoy!

While there is tea, there is hope.
—Sir Arthur Pinero

Tea lovers tell us an old-fashioned Brown Betty teapot guarantees the best tasting brew. The short, chubby shape of the teapot allows the tea leaves to gently swirl around as the boiling water is added, while the red terra cotta clay and Rockingham glaze cuddle the tea in a lasting warmth. They also suggest the Brown Betty seasons itself with each use creating more flavorful brews over time. (So take care not to use soap in your clean up. A good rinsing with hot water will do just fine!)

Lemon Curd

Use real butter and fresh lemon juice to make this extra tart and creamy

3 eggs   ½ cup lemon juice
1 cup sugar   ¼ cup butter, melted

In heavy saucepan, beat eggs and sugar. Stir in lemon juice and butter. Cook and stir over medium heat until mixture is thickened and it reaches 160-degrees. Cover and store in the refrigerator for up to one week. Serve with scones or tea biscuits.

Lemon curd is a popular and tasty spread, especially when served on scones. It can also be used as a filling for shortbreads or tarts.

A Prayer for Mother

Thank you for my mother's smile
That warmed my heart so true.
And thank you for her gentle strength
That always carried me through.

Thank you for my mother's arms
That held me when I cried.
And thank you for her loving praise
That made me glad I tried.

Thank you for my mother's love
And may she always know—
Dear Lord, I'm grateful every day
For her warm, sweet, loving soul.

Amen

A Bridal Tea

It's all about new beginnings!

Said the bride on the morning of her wedding, "Gotta go, my life is here!" Life arrives in a long white limousine, and she is off in a fairy princess dress to travel down the road of happy dreams and new beginnings.

To have a dream is to dance with the future.

Oh, what excitement! The making of a dream come true can be completely consuming - dare we say overwhelming? An intimate gathering for a bridal tea party is just what the bride-to-be needs! Amid the silk and lace, the florist and caterers, taking time out for tea is a great way to keep everything in perspective. What overwhelmed bride wouldn't relish some valuable moments of quiet reflection with friends?

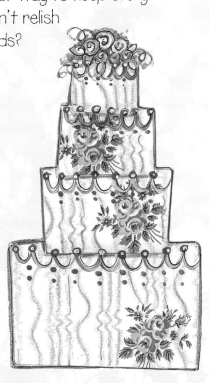

Taking a moments pause
for no reason than just—because.

Make the bride feel special. Treat her to tea and time alone with friends. When the big day arrives, along with the limousine, she'll have treasured memories of this gentle celebration tucked safely away in her heart.

Let the joy of this day be a joy
that will stay.

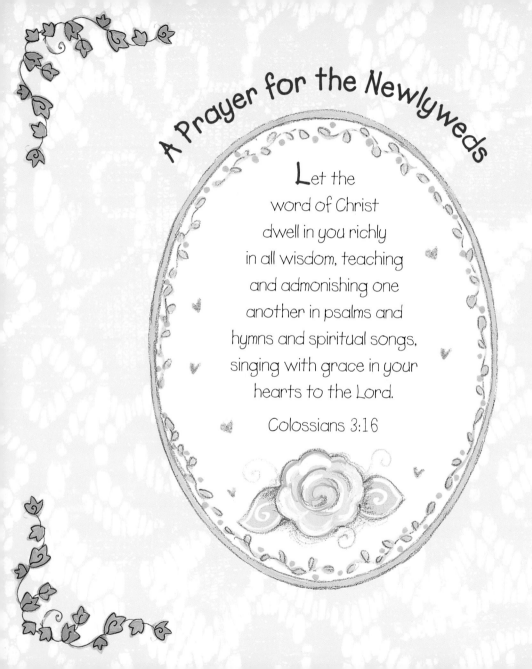

A Prayer for the Newlyweds

Let the
word of Christ
dwell in you richly
in all wisdom, teaching
and admonishing one
another in psalms and
hymns and spiritual songs,
singing with grace in your
hearts to the Lord.

Colossians 3:16

Gift Ideas for the Bride

Gift baskets with a kitchen theme are fun and functional. Line the basket with a colorful kitchen towel. Choose a recipe and include ingredients the bride will need to create the dish. Add some handy kitchen utensils and gadgets ... and don't forget the recipe!

Send blank recipe cards to guests along with the invitations and ask them to bring their favorite recipe to the tea party. Give the bride a recipe box and let guests add their recipe to the collection. What a clever, culinary treasure for the new bride!.

Teacups and saucers are a fun gift to give and a bridal tea is the perfect occasion. The bride may prefer a variety of cups and saucers or a matching set complete with cups, saucers, teapot, sugar and creamer, and tiered serving platter. Invite each guest to bring a piece of the collection as a gift for the bride, who will take home both lovely memories and everything she needs for a tea party of her own!

These delicious Cream Puff Shells stuffed with chicken salad
will have everyone smiling with delight!

Cream Puff Shells

½ cup butter   1 cup flour   4 eggs

1 cup water   ¼ tsp. salt

In saucepan, combine butter and water. Bring to a vigorous boil.
Reduce heat to low. Add flour and salt. Stir until mixture forms a stiff ball.
Remove from heat. Add eggs one at a time and stir well.
Spoon mixture in decorating bag with a large star
tip and make two-inch shells. Bake at 325-degrees
for 25 minutes. Cool.

Fancy Chicken Salad

2 cups finely chopped cooked chicken

1/2 cup finely chopped celery

salt and pepper to taste

3/4 cup mayonnaise

2 hard-boiled eggs, chopped

minced onion to taste

Combine all ingredients and mix well. Fill cream puff shells with mixture and chill.

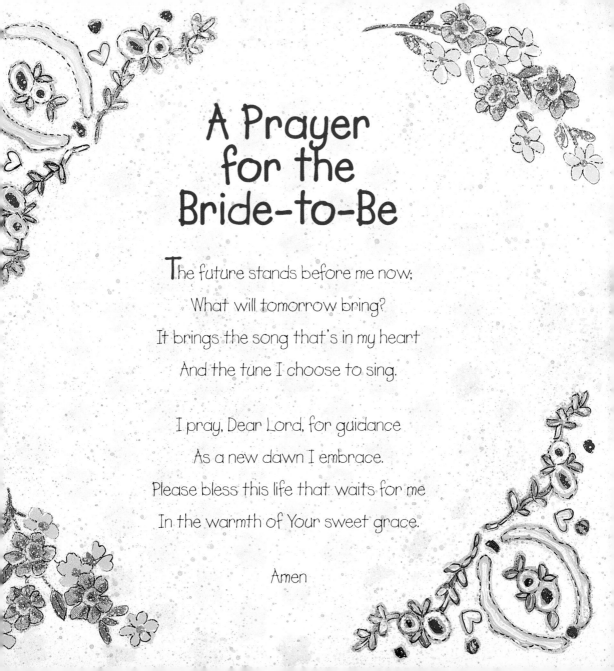

A Prayer
for the
Bride-to-Be

The future stands before me now;

What will tomorrow bring?

It brings the song that's in my heart

And the tune I choose to sing.

I pray, Dear Lord, for guidance

As a new dawn I embrace.

Please bless this life that waits for me

In the warmth of Your sweet grace.

Amen

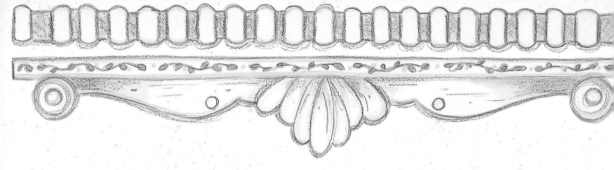

Hawaiian Wedding Cake

1 pkg. yellow cake mix.
1 can mandarin oranges (11 oz.)
1 can crushed pineapple (20 oz.)

Prepare cake mix as directed but add the oranges in place of the water. Bake as directed. Cool completely. Spread the crushed pineapple over the top of cake.

Icing:
1 large container of whipped topping
1 small package of vanilla instant pudding.
$^{1}/_{2}$ to 1 cup sweetened coconut

Mix whipped topping and pudding. Spread mixture over the crushed pineapple and top with coconut. This recipe can be made into a layered cake as well.

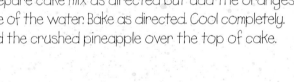

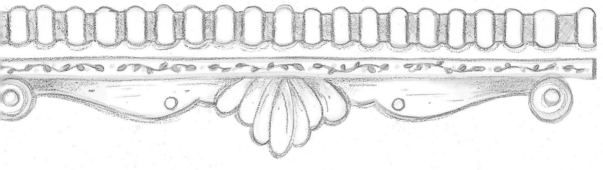

Ribbon Pulling

This charming tradition dates back to the time of Queen Victoria. A variety of small charms attached to ribbons were hidden in the icing of the cake as it was frosted and the ribbons fell gently down the sides of the cake. At the bridal shower, attendants and other friends of the bride each chose a ribbon and pulled it out of the cake to discover the hidden charm.

This is a fun way for the bride to present her attendants with a keepsake gift. In addition to the charms, the bride can present her attendants with charm bracelets or chains. The guide below explains what various charms symbolize:

Anchor—a life of stability

Baby booties—many healthy children

Church—next to be married

Compass—you let the Lord guide you

Cross—a life full of peace

Heart—your love is true

Musical note—harmonious home

Rose—a life of beauty

Teacup—life overflowing with joy

Teapot—life filled with warmth and hospitality

Wedding Traditions

The tradition of the bridal shower began when a seventeenth century Dutch maiden fell in love with a miller. Due to his generous tendencies of giving away flour to the poor, the miller lacked the sufficient financial means to marry. Local popularity for the couple prompted the community to "shower" them with the household goods they needed to start a life together so the maiden's father would consent to the marriage.

A wedding handkerchief is often passed from mother to daughter through the generations. The handkerchief is a symbol of the bride who cries at her wedding but will never shed another tear over her marriage.

An ancient Polish custom was to sprinkle sugar on the bride's bouquet to keep her disposition sweet.

The tradition of throwing rice at weddings was born from the belief that rice was the symbol of fruitfulness and prosperity, and tossing it on the bride and groom would bestow fertility upon them.

Love
always protects,
always trusts,
always hopes,
always
perseveres.
1 Corinthians
13:7

A Baby Shower Tea

It's all about CHANGE!

A new life is on the way … along with plenty of changes! Changing priorities, changing body shapes, changes in sleeping and eating habits, and changing diapers—lots and lots of diapers!

Life is precious
Life is sweet
Life is God's
Greatest treat.

And some things never change. Mommies deserve to be loved. So why not pamper the Mommie-to-Be with her very own tea party? Treat her to a special celebration of the new life she brings. Give her the gift of tender memories to keep wrapped up in her heart.

As the gifts are opened, what woman in her right mind can resist the opportunity to pass around soft, snuggly baby clothes, tiny toys and rattles, or handmade quilts and blankets? And, oh my goodness, we all know what those baby powder smells do to our hearts! These precious moments are priceless memories you can give to a friend.

Baby Shower Games

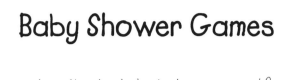

This game is quite simple, but always good for a few laughs. Pass around a roll of ribbon and let each guest cut off the amount they think will fit perfectly around the pregnant mommie's tummy. Whoever is closest, wins!

This game of memory will liven up the party. Place a large assortment of baby items, big and small, in a diaper bag. Pass the bag around and allow each guest fifteen seconds to look inside. Take the bag away and allow one minute for everyone to write down as many of the items in the bag as they can remember. Whoever remembers the most correct items wins and the diaper bag and goodies go to the guest of honor!

The table's all set
With lots of pretty things.
The kettle's on the stove
And soon will sing.
We're all gathered 'round
For a warm friendly tea,
And to enjoy one another
So delightfully!

Here's a nice way to gather valuable advice from experienced parents and create a warm memory for the expecting mother. Pass out colorful note cards to guests and have them write down their favorite child-rearing tip. Make sure they include their name and then have them pose for a picture. Place the note cards along with the corresponding photo in a photo album for the honored guest.

The term "nursery tea" in English tradition, referred to the evening meal for children. It was usually served at 4:00 P.M. in the nursery, as children did not dine with their parents.

Every baby born into the world
is a finer one than the last.
–Charles Dickens

Baby Shower Menu

Delicate Olive Cream Cheese Sandwiches

Spinach Salad with Strawberries

Front Porch Scones

Farmhouse Strawberry Jam

Ginger Peach Tea

Lemon Curd

Fresh Cream

Aunt Marie's Brownies

Cream Cheese Mints

Niceties

Elegant details create a party of distinction

- Wrap silverware with decorative cloth napkins then tie with a ribbon.

- Set fresh flower bouquets at each table in crystal or cut glass vases. Fresh greenery, ivy, and herbs are nice additions to trays of treats.

- Indirect lighting will create a more comfortable relaxed environment. Lamps and candles will soften the room visually.

- A shear fabric like tulle can be draped behind a gift table or other areas. Little twinkle lights or Christmas lights are pretty underneath the fabric.

- Set out a subtle fruity scented bowl of potpourri; peach is a soft fragrance.

- Describe teas and treats to guests before serving.

- Create a lovely bouquet for the mommy-to-be using a variety of flowers that have distinctive meanings. Attach a card with the meanings of the flowers. Here are some ideas:

Pink Carnation—maternal love and beauty

Lavender—devotion ☆ **Lamb's Ear**—softness

Lilac—sweetness ☆ **Lemon Balm**—love

Diaper Mint Cups

These little dandies are quick and easy to make and well worth the effort for the charm (and goodies).

Items needed:
- ☆ Five inch square of baby flannel
- ☆ Heavy starch (spray or liquid)
- ☆ Small gold safety pins

Each five inch square of baby flannel will make one mint cup. After cutting the needed amount of flannel squares, one at a time, spray (or dip) with the heavy starch. Fold the square into a triangle and then bring the three points together. Pin with a small gold safety pin. Shape the diaper into a fully open position and place on waxed paper to stiffen and dry. When completely dry, fill with mints, nuts or any other desired array of goodies.

① 　 ② FOLD ↓ 　 ③ Bring points together and pin.

This is the most unique cake you will ever see at a baby shower.
It makes a sensational centerpiece!

Diaper Cake

- ♡ 48 count disposable diapers
- ⭐ 2 spools ¼" × 18 ½ yds. ribbon
- ⭐ 5 yds. 1" wide ribbon
- ♡ Stuffed animal
- ⭐ Assorted baby items
     (pacifier, socks, teething ring, rattles)
- ⭐ 16" cardboard circle
- ♡ Receiving blanket

Cut the narrow ribbon in nine to ten inch lengths. Roll up the diapers and tie a ribbon around each one. Group seven diapers together and tie with ribbon. Add another ring around the first one and tie. Repeat this process one more time. Your first layer should have thirty-three diapers. For the second layer, group six diapers and tie together with ribbon. Add another ring with the remaining diapers. Wrap the cardboard with a receiving blanket. Place the first layer of diapers on top of the cardboard followed by the second layer. Decorate the cake with the baby items you have purchased, securing with ribbon. Place the stuffed animal on top of your cake. Wrap entire cake with the one-inch ribbon to hold everything in place.

Fresh Spinach SALAD with Strawberries

Make the dressing the day before your party.

Dressing:

1/2 cup canola oil

1/4 cup cider vinegar

1/4 tsp. worchestershire sauce

1/2 cup sugar

1/4 tsp. paprika

1 1/2 tsp. grated onion (optional)

3-4 strawberries mashed

Salad:

12 oz. fresh spinach leaves

1 qt. sliced strawberries

1/2 cup toasted almonds

Mix salad ingredients, toss with dressing, and serve. Raspberries and feta cheese can be substituted for the strawberries and almonds.

—Delores

These lovely mints will be the perfect touch for a baby shower.
No one can resist the creamy, melt-in-your-mouth refreshing taste!

Cream Cheese Mints

1 package powdered sugar (32 ounces)
1 package cream cheese, softened (8 ounces)
1 tsp. peppermint flavoring

food coloring (optional)
candy molds

Cream together powdered sugar and cream cheese in bowl. Add flavoring and food coloring and knead until consistency of pie dough. Keep unused mixture covered so it does not dry out. Form dough into half-inch balls, roll in sugar, and press into candy molds. Remove and store in container with wax paper in between layers. These can be made ahead of time and frozen.

A child fills
an empty spot
you didn't know
was there,
with dreams,
hope, happiness
and
tender loving
care

Be glad for all God is planning for you.
Be patient and prayerful always. Romans 12:12

A Blessing for Baby

Lord keep safe this little one
That's in our hearts so dear.
Guide us with your loving strength
As the day of birth grows near.

Please help this little baby
Make it safely, Lord, we pray—
Into our arms, into our hearts
Into our everyday.

Amen

A Birthday Tea
It's all about miracles!

Butterflies are beautiful symbols of the miracle of life.
What could be a better theme for a little girl's birthday tea party?

Butterfly, butterfly,
Miracle in flight.
Little girl, little girl,
Heavenly delight!

Fill that special little girl's day (and her memories)
with the delights of colorful flowers,
fluttering butterflies, and giggly friends.
Take lots of pictures!

What do I see from my windowsill?
The cheerful yellow smile of a daffodil.
A butterfly drifting of its own free will –
God's gentle beauty in its finest frill.

Cambric Tea

"Cambric tea was hot water and milk, with only a taste of tea in it, but little girls felt grown-up when their mothers let them drink cambric tea."

—Laura Ingalls Wilder, THE LONG WINTER

Little girls may not enjoy the full-bodied taste of brewed tea, so consider making Cambric tea for their party.

Cambric tea was served to children in the late nineteenth and early twentieth centuries. It consisted of a mixture of hot milk and water with a little sugar and a small amount of tea. The name comes from cambric fabric, which is thin and white.

These darling little butterfly cookies will flutter right into the theme of the birthday tea party. Caution: it may be necessary to have a butterfly net handy to keep them from disappearing too quickly!

Butterfly Sugar Cookies

1 cup sugar	1 cup butter	2 eggs
2 Tbsp. Milk	2 tsp. vanilla	3 cups flour
1 1/2 tsp. baking soda	1/2 tsp. baking powder	
1 tsp. cream of tartar	1/2 tsp. salt	

Cream sugar, butter, and eggs together until fluffy. Add remaining ingredients and chill several hours. Roll dough on floured surface to one quarter inch thickness. Cut with a butterfly shaped cookie cutter. Bake at 350-degrees for 8 minutes. Remove to wire rack and cool completely.

Icing:

Cook 4 1/2 Tbsp. sugar and 2 Tbsp. water until they form a syrup, being careful not to let it crystalize. Let the syrup cool. Beat 2 1/3 cups powdered sugar, 1 egg, a pinch of salt, and 1 1/2 tsp. vanilla. Add 1/2 cup shortening and the syrup and beat on high for 10 minutes. Divide into batches and create a variety of colors using food coloring. Spread on cooled cookies.

A Game of Musical Butterflies

This game is like musical chairs but with a different twist. Prior to your party, find a butterfly trinket that can easily be held in a child's hand or create a paper butterfly of your own. Have all the birthday guests stand in a circle. Someone will need to be in charge of playing the music (maybe "Butterfly Kisses"). When the music starts, the butterfly is passed from person to person clockwise. When the music stops, the person standing to the left of the person holding the butterfly is out of the game. The game continues until the last person remains holding the butterfly. The winner keeps the trinket and then passes out other prizes to the remaining players!

Looking for a unique birthday gift?
This sweet poem can be copied and tied with
a ribbon to a miniature tea set!

A tiny little tea set
Just for me.
Tiny cups and saucers
And a teapot so wee.

Pink and purple flowers
Are painted on the side,
With tiny green leaves
Where the flowers try to hide.

I keep it on a little shelf
Just right for me to see—
Tiny cups and saucers
And a teapot just for me.

Thank God for tea!
What would the world do without it?
–Sydney Smith

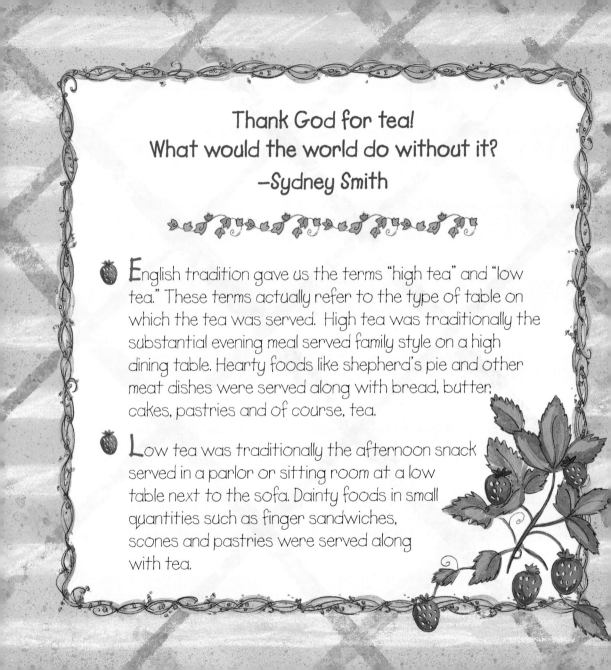 English tradition gave us the terms "high tea" and "low tea." These terms actually refer to the type of table on which the tea was served. High tea was traditionally the substantial evening meal served family style on a high dining table. Hearty foods like shepherd's pie and other meat dishes were served along with bread, butter, cakes, pastries and of course, tea.

Low tea was traditionally the afternoon snack served in a parlor or sitting room at a low table next to the sofa. Dainty foods in small quantities such as finger sandwiches, scones and pastries were served along with tea.

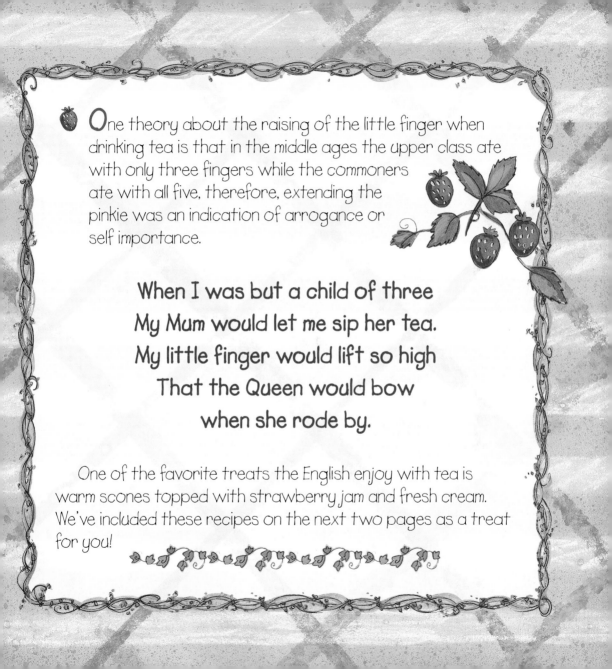

One theory about the raising of the little finger when drinking tea is that in the middle ages the upper class ate with only three fingers while the commoners ate with all five, therefore, extending the pinkie was an indication of arrogance or self importance.

When I was but a child of three
My Mum would let me sip her tea.
My little finger would lift so high
That the Queen would bow
when she rode by.

One of the favorite treats the English enjoy with tea is warm scones topped with strawberry jam and fresh cream. We've included these recipes on the next two pages as a treat for you!

Front Porch Scones

2 cups all-purpose flour
4 Tbsp. brown sugar
2 tsp. baking powder
½ tsp. baking soda
½ tsp. salt
⅓ cup butter, cold

1 carton sour cream (8 oz.)
1 beaten egg yolk
1 beaten egg white
1 Tbsp. water
1 Tbsp. brown sugar
¼ tsp. cinnamon

In a mixing bowl, combine the dry ingredients. Using a pastry blender, cut in cold butter until mixture resembles course crumbs. Mix sour cream and egg yolk together. Add to the dry ingredients, stirring with a fork until moist. On lightly floured surface, knead dough gently ten to twelve strokes. Roll dough to one-half inch thick and cut with a biscuit cutter. Place scones on a baking sheet and cut each into four wedges but do not separate the wedges. Brush tops of scones with egg white and water mixture. Combine cinnamon and brown sugar and sprinkle on top of each scone. Bake in a 425-degree oven for ten minutes. Remove from baking sheet and cool slightly. Break scones apart into wedges and serve warm.

Farmhouse Strawberry JAM

5 cups crushed strawberries   7 cups sugar
1 box fruit pectin   1/2 tsp. butter

Wash berries, discard stems and blemishes, and crush berries, 1 cup at a time. Measure sugar in a separate bowl (do not reduce sugar). Stir fruit pectin into fruit and add butter. Bring mixture to full rolling boil, stirring constantly. Stir in sugar quickly and return to full rolling boil. Boil for one minute. Remove from heat and skim off any foam. Pour into prepared jars and fill to within one eighth inch of top. After jam has cooled, pour a thin coat of paraffin wax to seal and place in freezer. Thaw in refrigerator when ready to enjoy.

FRESH CREAM

2 cups heavy whipping cream   3/4 tsp. cream of tartar
2/3 cup powdered sugar   1 tsp. vanilla

Beat all ingredients with a mixer until stiff. Refrigerate and serve with scones and jam.

May all your dreams have their day.

No matter how you spend your day—
Hope it's great in every way!

For the goodness you've shared in so many ways.

May an abundance of blessings
come to you on this day.

A Birthday Prayer

Thank You for another year
Of good health, love and laughter.
I pray Your guiding hands will stay,
With me now and ever after.

Amen

A Christmas Tea
It's all about FAITH!

Christmas is a time to share the faith we hold close in our hearts. It's a season of joy and love.

**Rejoice in the season and all of its grace.
Take heart in the blessings of comfort and faith.**

Christmas is such festive fun! It's the perfect time to share your faith in fellowship with friends. A Christmas Tea just might be one of the best ways to celebrate the season. Gather friends and family around a perfectly brewed pot of tea along with your favorite Christmas goodies. We guarantee happy hearts and faces!

**Shout to the tall, shout to the small
Great tidings of Christmas
for one and for all!**

Let your faith pour out as warmly as the tea. Fill the room with aromas of love, faith, and sugar cookies! Treat this gleeful gathering as a tribute to the good gifts God has given—especially the gift of His Son.

A Christmas Cookie Tea Party

Who can resist the wonderful variety of cookies that appear everywhere at Christmas? It's such fun to make the cookies and even more fun to share them. So why not have a cookie exchange tea party?

Ask each guest to bring two to four dozen of their favorite holiday cookies to exchange with other guests. Your guests will not only enjoy a delicious tea party but will take home a delicious variety of cookies to enjoy throughout the season.

A true friend warms by her presence and remembers you in her prayers.
–Anonymous

Shortbread Cookies

1 1/2 cups butter softened

1/2 cup sugar

2 tsp. almond flavoring

1 egg white

2 tsp. cinnamon

4 cups all purpose flour

4 Tbsp. sugar

1/2 - 1 cup finely chopped almonds

Cream butter and sugar. Stir in flavoring and flour. Mix well. Cover and chill overnight. Roll out on a lightly floured surface to one-quarter inch thickness. Cut with cookie cutters and place on cookie sheets. Beat egg white until foamy and brush lightly over cookies. Mix cinnamon and sugar together and sprinkle mixture over cookies. Top with almonds. Bake at 350-degrees for 8 minutes or until lightly browned. Cool on wire racks.

Christmas Tea Party Menu

Scrumptious Chocolate
Caramel Squares

Christmas
Fruit Salad

Chocolate
Nut Clusters

Divinity

Hot Peach
Tea

Christmas Party Prayer

With joyous hearts we gather 'round,
Our hearts are filled with faith.
We pray, dear Lord, that You will hold
Our souls in Your embrace.
In fellowship we all join hands
To share and celebrate
The wondrous lives You've given us
and blessed with all Your grace.
Amen

Here's a sweet treat for a sweet occasion.
Add red or green Jell-O to make the candy more colorful!

Divinity

4 cups sugar

1 cup white syrup

4 egg whites, beaten stiff

1 tsp. vanilla

$^1/_2$ tsp. salt

1 cup boiling water

$^1/_2$ package strawberry Jell-O

In a heavy saucepan, stir sugar, syrup, water, and salt. Once this mixture reaches a strong boil, don't stir very often. Boil until syrup reaches 260-degrees. Pour one cup of the syrup over the egg whites and beat in. Cook the remaining syrup until it reaches 280-degrees. Slowly pour over egg whites. Beat by hand until it begins to thicken or looses its gloss. Add strawberry Jell-O and vanilla. Pour into a 9 x 13 inch greased pan or drop by spoonfuls on wax paper.

This quick tea mix is an inviting cup
of warmth on a cold day.
You might even call it comfort in a cup!

Easy Hot Peach Tea

1 1/2 cup sugar

1/2 cup orange breakfast drink mix

1/2 cup instant tea

4 packages peach Jell-O

    (or raspberry if you prefer)

1 large package pre-sweetened lemonade

Mix all ingredients together and store in an air-tight container. Mix three to four teaspoons per cup of hot water for a flavorful tea. The dry mixture makes a wonderful Christmas gift. Attach the recipe to the jar with a festive ribbon.

Scrumptious Chocolate Caramel Squares

xxxxxxxxxxxx xxxxxxx xxxxxxxx

14 oz. bag caramels

1 German chocolate cake mix

1 cup chopped nuts

$2/3$ cup evaporated milk, divided

$3/4$ cup butter, melted

1 cup chocolate chips

Combine 1/3 cup evaporated milk and caramels in heavy pan. Stir constantly over low heat until caramels are melted. Set aside. In large bowl, combine cake mix, butter, 1/3 cup evaporated milk and nuts. Stir by hand until dough holds together. Pat 1/2 of mixture in 9 x 13 inch greased pan. Bake at 350-degrees for 6 minutes. Spread caramel mixture over baked crust. Sprinkle chips over caramel. Crumble remaining dough over caramel mixture. Return to oven 15-18 minutes. Cool.

You can't get a cup of tea large enough
or a book long enough to suit me.
—C. S. Lewis

Christmas Fruit Salad

1 can cherry pie filling
1 small can crushed pineapple, well drained
1 can sweetened condensed milk
1 1/2 cups miniature marshmallows
1 carton whipped topping (8 ounces)
1 small pkg. pecan pieces

Mix in order given. Chill. Serves 10-12.

Chocolate Nut Clusters

2 cups chocolate chips   2 tsp. butter flavored shortening
2 cups chopped pecans, cashews or walnuts

In microwave-safe bowl, melt chips and shortening on high for two minutes or until smooth when stirred. Stir in nuts. Spoon into paper lined mini muffin cups and fill 3/4 full.

Chill until firm.

Glory to God
and let peace guide the way
To the love and celebration
Of a joyous Christmas day.

And she brought forth her firstborn son,
and wrapped Him in swaddling cloths,
and laid Him in a manger,
because there was no room for them in the inn. . . .
Glory to God in the highest,
and on earth peace,
goodwill toward men!

Luke 2:7, 14

We love
because
God first loved us.

1 John 4:19

May a star of shining hope
glow brightly
for your Christmas.

Rosy cheeks and crispy air—
Cheery hearts are everywhere.
Children raise their voice to sing
In praise of all
that Christmas brings.

Thanks be to God
for His indescribable gift!
2 Corinthians 9:15

These empty pages are waiting to be filled with *joyous* accounts of laughter and fun, gentle conversation, good tea, and warm memories. Take a few moments to record the special memories of your very own "Teatime Treasures."

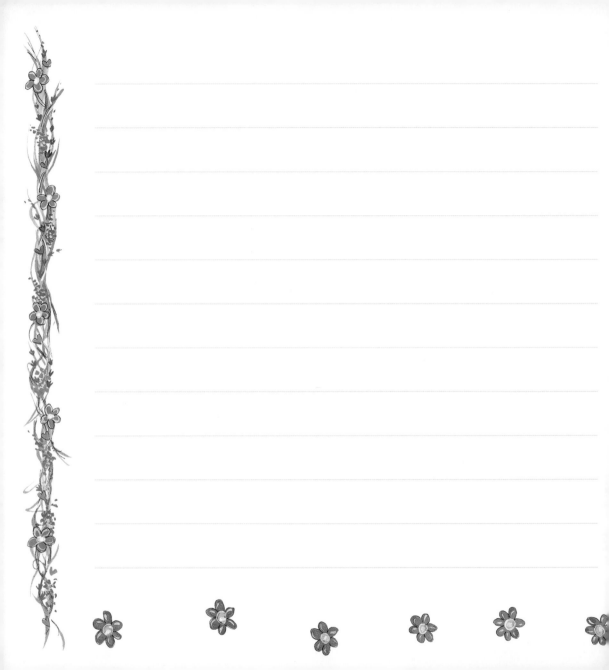

Develop a passion for tea.
It happened to me
So easily,
And now you see
The calm in me
Is from the glee
Of sipping tea.
Yes, I've become a devotee
To the lovely pleasure that tea can be.
Develop a passion for tea!